Joe's nose

Story written by Liz Miles
Illustrated by Tim Archbold

Speed Sounds

Consonants *Ask children to say the sounds.*

f	l	m	n	r	s	v	z	sh	th	ng
ff	ll	mm	nn	rr	ss	ve	zz			nk
ph	le	mb	kn	**wr**	se		se			
			gn		**c**		**s**			
					ce					

b	c	d	g	h	j	p	qu	t	w	x	y	ch
bb	k	dd	gg		g	pp		tt	wh			**tch**
	ck		gu		ge							
					dge							

Each box contains one sound but sometimes more than one grapheme.
*Focus graphemes for this story are **circled**.*

4

Vowels

Ask children to say the sounds in and out of order.

a	e ea	i	o	u	ay a͡-e a	ee ea y e	igh i͡-e ie i	ow o-e o oe
at	hen	in	on	up	day	see	high	blow

oo u͡-e ue	oo	ar	or oor ore aw	air are	ir ur er	ou ow	oy oi
zoo	look	car	for	fair	whirl	shout	boy

Story Green Words

Ask children to read the words first in Fred Talk and then say the word.

clothes   hose   spoke   wife   doze   Joe   hurt*   whose*

Ask children to say the syllables and then read the whole word.

take|a|way   week|end   a|bout   bas|ket   un|til   so|fa
To|by   groc|er|ies*

Ask children to read the root first and then the whole word with the suffix.

rose → roses   nod → nodded   struggle → struggled

brag → bragged   job → jobs   get → getting   lie → lied

happen → happening   grow → grows   long → longer*

* Challenge Words

Vocabulary Check

Discuss the meaning (as used in the story) after the children have read each word.

	definition:	sentence:
chores	little jobs at home	... Joe and his wife, Anya, had lots of chores to do.
groceries	food shopping	Anya had to go shopping for groceries.
doze	sleep for a short time	... all he wanted to do was to doze and play football.
twitched	moved suddenly	Joe's nose twitched.
snoozed	had a short sleep	Mrs Lee piled the clothes in the basket as Joe snoozed.
effort	hard work	Cooking lunch was too much effort, so he rang for a takeaway.
bragged	showed off	It was fine until his mate bragged, "I went for a long run this morning."

Red Words

Ask children to practise reading the words across the rows, down the columns and in and out of order clearly and quickly.

old	all	could	are
water	my	through	son
want	one	ball	whole
people	now	once	anyone
over	was	two	some

Joe's nose

It was the weekend and Joe and his wife, Anya, had lots of chores to do. Anya had to go shopping for groceries. Joe had jobs too, but all he wanted to do was to doze and play football.

Joe lay on the sofa and looked at his list of chores. First he needed to water the roses.

"Toby, I've twisted my wrist," Joe lied to his son.
"Will you water the roses for me?"

Toby nodded. Joe's nose itched.

As Toby struggled with the wriggly hose, Joe dozed.

Next on the list was getting the clothes in.

Joe spotted Mrs Lee next door.
"I've got a bad back, Mrs Lee. Please will you get the clothes off our line too?" he asked.

Joe's nose twitched.

Mrs Lee piled the clothes in the basket as Joe snoozed.

Then Joe needed to make lunch.

Cooking lunch was too much effort, so he rang for a takeaway.

"I've cooked lunch," Joe lied to Anya. And then his nose wiggled so much he ran to look in the mirror.

"Oh no! What's happening to my nose?" he gasped.

At football, Joe tried to hide his nose with his hand.

It was fine until his mate bragged, "I went for a long run this morning."

Joe said, "Me too!" and felt his nose grow. Now it was too long to hide.

Joe panicked and tried to run away, but he tripped on the ball.

"What's happened to your nose?" Anya asked, when Joe got home.

Suddenly Joe realised what had happened: "I told some lies, and each time I lied my nose got longer and longer!

I said I had a bad wrist... but I didn't.
I said I had a bad back... but I didn't.
I said I cooked lunch... but I didn't.
I said I went for a run... but I didn't.

Then I tripped up. This time my back really does hurt!"

As he spoke, Joe's nose started to itch one more time. It began to shrink and soon it was back to the right size!

Toby sat next to Joe. "Daddy, please read this book to me. It's the one about a boy whose nose grows when he tells lies!"

Questions to talk about

Ask children to TTYP each question using 'Fastest finger' (FF) or 'Have a think' (HaT).

p.9   (FF)   What was the first job on Joe's list?

pp.10–11 (HaT)   Why did Joe lie to Toby and then to Mrs Lee?

p.12   (HaT)   Why was Joe's nose growing?

p.14   (FF)   Which one of Joe's lies became true?

p.15   (HaT)   What made Joe's nose shrink back to its usual size?

p.15   (FF)   What book does Toby want to read?

Questions to read and answer

(Children complete without your help.)

1. **Anya / Toby / Mrs Lee** watered the roses for Joe.

2. When Mrs Lee was getting the clothes in, Joe **snoozed / helped / cooked lunch**.

3. When Joe looked in the mirror he saw that his nose **had shrunk / was the right size / had grown**.

4. Joe's mate told him that he had **been for a long run / watered the roses / hurt his wrist**.

5. Joe **kicked the football / was hit by the football / tripped on the football** when he tried to run away.

Speedy Green Words

Ask children to practise reading the words across the rows, down the columns and in and out of order clearly and quickly.

boy	nose	started	grows
right	away	please	door
too	read	home	hide
more	about	book	play
our	line	weekend	rang